THE RAINBOW AND YOU

written by
E.C. KRUPP

illustrated by
ROBIN RECTOR KRUPP

HarperCollinsPublishers

*To Foster William Krupp,
where our rainbow begins*

The Rainbow and You
Text copyright © 2000 by E. C. Krupp.
Illustrations copyright © 2000 by Robin Rector Krupp.

Printed in Singapore at Tien Wah Press.
All rights reserved.
http://www.harperchildrens.com

Library of Congress Cataloging-in-Publication Data
Krupp, E. C. (Edwin C.).
The rainbow and you / E. C. Krupp; illustrated by Robin
Rector Krupp.
p. cm.
Summary: Explains how rainbows are formed by the colors
in sunlight shining through raindrops.
ISBN 0-688-15601-0 (trade)—ISBN 0-688-15602-9 (library)
1. Rainbow Juvenile literature. [1. Rainbow.] I. Krupp,
Robin Rector, ill. II. Title. QC976.R2K78 2000 551.56'7—
dc21 99-34337 CIP

10 9 8 7 6 5 4 3 2
❖

Some people say there is a pot of gold at the end of the rainbow, but it's never been found. The real treasure of the rainbow is its colors.

Have you ever tried to walk under a rainbow? You can't, and you can't touch a rainbow, either. That doesn't mean rainbows aren't real. It just means they aren't solid. Rainbows are actually light. You can only catch one with your eyes.

Most of the time people say the rainbow has seven colors—red, orange, yellow, green, blue, indigo, and violet. You can remember the colors with this sentence:

Run Onto Your Gold Before It Vanishes.
Red, Orange, Yellow, Green, Blue, Indigo, Violet

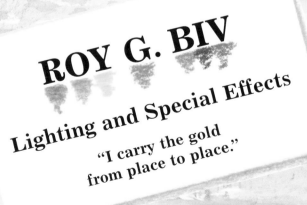

ROY G. BIV

Lighting and Special Effects

"I carry the gold
from place to place."

ROY G. BIV gets his name from the seven colors of the rainbow. He is a rainbow expert. He knows all about lighting and special effects. Some people use his name to remember the colors.

The rainbow gets its name from its shape and from the weather that makes it happen. Long ago, people thought the rainbow looked like a bow for shooting arrows. Because they saw this bow of color only when it had been raining, they called it the rainbow.

It takes more than rain to make a rainbow, however. It also takes sunshine. Whenever you look at a rainbow, the sun is behind you. The falling raindrops, in the distance in front of you, are like a movie screen. Sunlight hits the raindrop screen, and the rainbow appears in full color.

You are here.

The ancient Greeks noticed the way rainbows come and go and said the rainbow travels with a messenger from the gods. They called her Iris and said she flies along the rainbow's colorful bridge between heaven and earth. She magically lifts water from the earth into the clouds, and it falls as rain.

The Vikings
believed a rainbow
bridge connected Asgard,
the sky kingdom of the high
gods, with Midgard, the earth
below. Asgard was supported
in the heavens by the branches of
the World Tree. The god Heimdall
guarded the rainbow from giants
who lived at the edge of the sky.

Monument Valley,
Arizona,
United States

The Navajo of the American Southwest say
Monster Slayer and Born for Water, the twin hero
sons of the sun, journeyed to their father's world
by stepping onto the rainbow.

Ayers Rock, or Uluru,
Australia

In Siberia people said the rainbow was the storm
god's bow, and with it he shot arrows of lightning
through the sky.

Australian tribes know the rainbow as the great
serpent of the Dreamtime. That was the time, they
say, when the world was created.

Noah's Ark

Mount Ararat,
Turkey

In the Bible, the rainbow signals the
end of the rain and is God's promise the
world will not be destroyed again by flood.
Because it takes broken clouds to let the
sunlight fall against the rain, rainbows
usually do tell us the rain is ending.

SUNLIGHT

There is a rainbow of color in your box of crayons, but some of those crayons have colors you'll never see in a rainbow. You probably have a black crayon, but black is not really a color. We see black when there is no light, and when there is no light, there is no color. Browns, grays, and other hues are mixtures that sunlight can't put into the rainbow.

Isaac Newton is the scientist who explained the rainbow. He also discovered the law of gravity, which explains why raindrops fall. Newton showed that sunlight is really made of the rainbow's colors. When those colors are all mixed together, we call it white light. Newton bent the sunlight with a wedge of glass called a prism and made a rainbow out of sunlight in a darkened room. He then sent that rainbow through another prism and combined the colors back into white light. That proved the rainbow was in the sunlight.

Isaac Newton was born in 1642 and died in 1727.

How can raindrops spread sunlight into all those colors? They bend the light. Raindrops are water, and water can bend light. In the air, all of the colors in the sunlight travel together in the same direction. When they enter the raindrop, the colors separate as they bend in different directions.

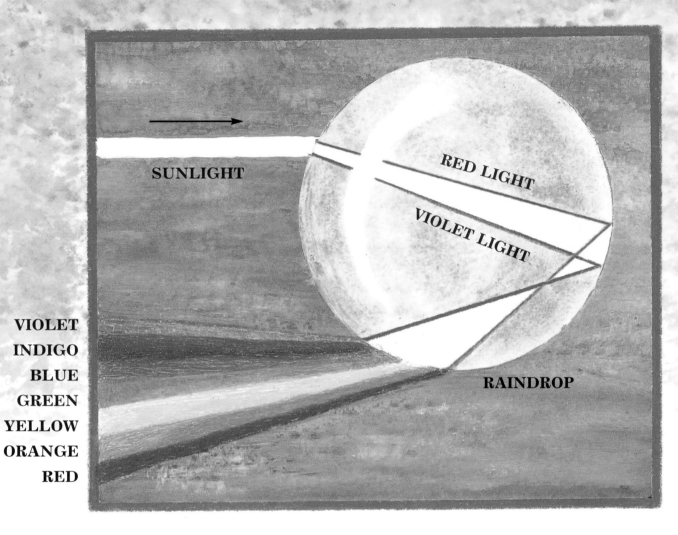

SUNLIGHT

RED LIGHT

VIOLET LIGHT

RAINDROP

VIOLET
INDIGO
BLUE
GREEN
YELLOW
ORANGE
RED

Violet light bends the most. Red light bends the least. Each color bends differently. That's why each color is headed in a slightly different direction when it leaves the raindrop.

The back of the raindrop works like a mirror. Inside the raindrop, most of the sunlight is bent and bounced back to the front of the drop, where the light entered. By then, the light is aimed back toward the ground in the sun's direction. If you are in the right place, you will see some of that light as a rainbow.

When you see a single rainbow, red is always on the outside of the arc, and violet is on the inside.

Some of the sunlight in a raindrop bounces twice before it leaves the drop, and that light can add a second rainbow above the first.

In a double rainbow, the outer rainbow is fainter. A little light is lost with each bounce. The second bounce also flips the colors. Their order in the second rainbow is reversed. Violet is on top, and red is on the bottom.

The world's largest natural arch—
Rainbow Bridge National Monument,
Utah, United States

By bending and bouncing sunlight, each raindrop makes its own rainbow, but that's not the rainbow you see. One drop makes only a tiny part of the rainbow. It takes millions of raindrops to steer the entire rainbow your way.

Of course, all of the raindrops are constantly falling. A raindrop beaming red light into your eye at one moment can't do that a moment later. By then, the raindrop is closer to the ground. It's in the wrong spot to put red color into your rainbow.

Red light from your rainbow comes from higher raindrops.

If red comes out at the bottom from the raindrop, why is red on the top of the rainbow?

Red light from lower raindrops misses your eyes.

Even though the raindrops keep falling, the rainbow doesn't have to disappear. If the rain continues, new drops replace the ones that slip away.

Each person sees a different rainbow. The rainbow rays that reach your eyes miss the rest of us. A person next to you is standing in a slightly different spot and sees a rainbow in a slightly different place. It looks the same, but it is made by other falling drops. So when the sun shines against the passing rain, there are plenty of rainbows to go around.

Rainbows usually last only
a few minutes, but you can
train yourself to be a good
eyewitness reporter. Before you
turn the page, try to notice as
many things as possible about
your rainbow.

Rainbow Reporting

What is the date and year?
What is the season?
Where are you?
What is the time?
How long did the rainbow last?
In what direction was the sun?
In what direction was the rainbow?
Was the sun high or low?
Was the rainbow high or low?
Was the rainbow complete?
Did it change?
Was it a single or a double rainbow?
In what order were the colors?
What about the sky on either side of
   the rainbow?
Could you see through the rainbow?

COMPLIMENTS OF ROY G. BIV ENTERPRISES

Rainbow Rules

Rainbows are always opposite the sun.

When the sun is low, the rainbow is high. The higher the sun, the lower the rainbow.

The sky is bright inside the rainbow and dark outside.

Some rays of light bounce out of the raindrops at other angles and add white light inside the bow.

The most rainbow you can see from flat ground is a semicircle. This would happen only at sunrise or sunset.

Viewed from an airplane or a very high mountain, a rainbow can be a complete circle.

In winter the raindrops freeze into snowflakes, and so we get fewer rainbows.

Rain forests and rainy tropical islands, like Hawaii, get rainbows more frequently.

Most of the raindrops
that make your rainbow are
about two miles away, but you
can make your own nearby
rainbow with a hose. Stand
with your back to the sun,
and spray in front of you.
That rainbow is right in
your own neighborhood.

Sometimes you can see
rainbow colors without the
bow. Oil on a puddle, CDs,
soap bubbles, pearls, and some
shells bring us rainbow colors
even when there's no rain.

Our world is the only planet in the solar system where rainbows are possible. The sun makes the earth just the right temperature to let water roll in the oceans, spray in the waves, pool in the lakes, run in the rivers, collect in the clouds, and fall as rain. Without that water, we wouldn't have rainbows.

Saturn

RAINBOW PATROL DEPUTY

RAINBOW PATROL
LIFETIME MEMBERSHIP
(Your name here)

Roy G. Biv
ROY G. BIV, Squad Leader

Since no one sees exactly the same rainbow, that rainbow you see belongs to you. Now that you know how to watch the rain and the sun, you belong to the Rainbow Patrol.